AF292548

ROT AND MOULD

By
Robin Twiddy

FOREST EXPLORER

BookLife
PUBLISHING

©2018
**BookLife Publishing
King's Lynn
Norfolk PE30 4LS**
All rights reserved.
Printed in Malaysia.

A catalogue record for this book is available from the British Library.

ISBN: 978-1-78637-479-0

Written by:
Robin Twiddy

Edited by:
Kirsty Holmes

Designed by:
Gareth Liddington

CONTENTS

Words that look like **this** can be found in the glossary on page 24.

LET'S EXPLORE

WELCOME, FOREST EXPLORER!

Welcome, forest explorer! Today we will be looking for rot and mould on the forest floor. We will learn where to look and how rot and mould help the forest.

A budding forest explorer will need:
GRAB YOUR EQUIPMENT
Sandwich Bag
Walking Boots
Magnifying Glass
Notebook

WHAT IS ROT?

Look at the floor – what do you see? Maybe dead leaves, soil or fallen sticks? If things did not rot, the forest would be full of fallen leaves and old branches.

Rotting is the forest's way of recycling.

All the old things in the forest will rot and **decay**.
When things rot, they **break down** and become part of the soil.

ROTTING THINGS

Have you ever picked up an old stick in the forest and found that it is soft and breaks easily? That is because it is rotting!

This tree trunk will take a long time to rot because it is big and **dense**.

WHAT HELPS ROT?

How warm and damp is it in the forest? Things rot faster when the **environment** is warm and damp. Mould helps speed up the rotting process.

WHAT IS MOULD?

Mould is part of the **fungi** family, just like mushrooms.
Moulds get their food from whatever they are growing on.

When mould grows on something, like an old branch, it helps to break it down. Moulds come in lots of colours: blue, black, red, green, white and pink.

This fruit has been covered in mould and is decomposing.

SLIME MOULD

Slime moulds are not fungi. They grow in the forest and can be very colourful. Slime moulds sometimes look like mushrooms and help things to rot.

Slime mould can move up to 2.5 centimetres (cm) a day!

Keep an eye out for slime mould. If you see some, write down what it looks like and where you saw it. Check in a day or two to see if it's moved!

SIGNS OF ROT

So forest explorer, how do you find something that is rotting?
First look out for mushrooms and fungi. Wood needs fungi
to help it rot.

Keep an eye open for warm, damp areas. Rot and mould love warmth and damp. You might find a rotting log or fallen leaves.

Your nose won't help you, because plant and tree rot doesn't smell!

TWIGS, TRUNKS AND ROT 'N' MOULD

Trees can take hundreds of years to completely rot away. If you find a fallen tree, it might have fallen when your grandparents were children – or before they were born!

When old leaves and fallen trees rot, they put lots of nutrients back into the soil. This helps the forest grow and stay healthy.

MAKE IT MOULDY

If you want to see how mould grows and how it helps things rot, you can try this mould experiment at home.

Place a piece of fruit into a sealable sandwich bag.
Sprinkle a little water onto it and seal the bag.
Place the bag in a warm place. Check the bag every two days.

Throw away your mould bag
after ten days without opening it.

KEEPING NOTES

Rot and mould are very important in the forest and help to bring new life to the other plants and creatures that live there.

GLOSSARY

break down	to be taken apart
decay	to rot or decompose
decompose	decay or rot
dense	tightly packed
environment	the natural surroundings
fungi	a type of life similar to plants but does not create food from sunlight – mushrooms, yeast and moulds are fungi
nutrients	natural substances that plants and animals need to grow and stay healthy
recycling	reusing materials for other purposes

INDEX